"I find this a very useful and practical book. [illegible] doing their own thing. I wish such a guide had been available when I was setting up my own business."

Keith Harrison
Special Professor, Nottingham University Business School
www.nottingham.ac.uk
Chairman Nottingham Climbing Centre
www.nottingham-climbing.co.uk

"This is one of those ideas that you wonder why no one has thought of before because there is such a clear need for it. I have never seen anything like it. This is superb. This guide is a user-friendly concise tool for really helping you decide on your future. In my work and personal life, I come across so many people at this crossroads who would benefit from the guide.

The practical guide really could change your life. It is certain to be a best seller."

Jo Derbyshire
Managing Director
Loughborough Innovation Centre
www.loughborough-enterprises.co.uk

"Cathy's book provides some excellent tools to help those planning self-employment or setting up their own company. The personal strength of character, drive and ambition of individuals and the quality of their new business idea underpin self-employed success. Yet they are frequently overlooked.

What Cathy provides through her logical and easy to read book is an essential evaluation tool, coupled with great practical tips on how to improve the essential qualities needed to flourish. Case studies clearly explain all the principles in practice which transforms the text from theory to an essential guide book – which will help the entrepreneur throughout their new venture.

I heartily recommend it to anyone considering self-employment."

Phil Marriott
TaxAssist Accountants (Loughborough) Ltd
Director
The Accountancy and Tax Service for Small Business
www.taxassist.co.uk/philmarriot

"I think this is an excellent guide and does exactly what is says on the tin, 'A Practical Guide'. The case studies are comprehensive and diverse and give an excellent flavour of the transition journey. The supporting notes bring out the practical steps and the beliefs and attitudes required to make this journey.

A great piece of practical professional advice."

Roger Bicknell
Managing Consultant
Career Management Consultants Ltd
www.cmc-careers.com

Consulting Services Limited   1

did you know?

- The number of people being self-employed has tripled in the last 20 years.
- In the last 20 years, the numbers becoming self-employed from manual occupations have increased by more than 450% and from managerial positions have increased by almost 300%.
- It is predicted that by 2010, over 30% of the UK population will be self-employed.

If you are thinking about going self-employed, you are not alone.

this practical guide may be useful for you, if:

- You have always dreamt of becoming your own boss.
- You have begun self-employment, but it is not working out as planned.
- You are self-employed and you are looking to reinvent yourself.

this practical guide aims to:

- Help you to move successfully into self-employment.
- If you are already self-employed and it isn't going to plan, support you in completing your own personal business health check.
- If you are already successfully self-employed, help you to start afresh with a new business.

This practical guide is a result of 18 months of research, from speaking to people who had successfully taken that step into self-employment. It is a summary of what they found worked.

this practical guide won't:

- Help you to write a business plan.
- Choose an accountant.
- Decide whether you should be a limited business or a sole trader.

There are many existing courses and books that can help you to do that. Some of these are listed in **Chapter 12. where to get more help.**

however, what this practical guide will do is to help you to:

- Create the momentum to move into self-employment.
- Prepare yourself so that you are poised to take your first steps.
- Physically get some of the essential arrangements in place.

Why reinvent the wheel? It makes sense to benefit from other people's experiences and luck!

CANNINGTON CENTRE

Processed: 04/09

Class: AVD CAREERS

Barcode: BO154630

with thanks

I wish to thank a number of people who have made this practical guide possible.

First and foremost I would like to express thanks for the research interviewees who contributed to the initial research findings. Little did we realise at the time that those interviews would lead to the creation of the Testing the Water™ questionnaire and this practical guide. Without you, this practical guide would not have been possible! - A big thank you to Rob Nathan, who has worked in partnership with me to translate the research findings into practical tools that can be of value to others. His experience and insights are greatly valued.

A warm thanks to Sue Ricks who has provided personal and practical support in copious quantities which has helped to make this practical guide a reality. This has especially been prevalent during our bi-annual writing sessions in the Peak District. Nicola Hancock has provided insights and useful feedback when reviewing this book. In addition, Jayne Thompson has helped to translate my draft into an accessible and readable form. A big thank you for this – no mean feat!

A special mention goes to Ian Fryer, who has been there alongside me on this writing journey. His calming influence and attention to detail has been immensely appreciated. Finally, I would like to recognise the support that I have received from my Mum and Dad. They have always been there and have supported me through sharing the wisdom of their experiences.

Cathy Brown 2008.

contents

chapter 1. setting the scene

As you may know, more and more people are moving into self-employment. If you read employment studies, the stats show that between 1987-1998, the number of professional and managerial people in the UK that have become self-employed has increased by over 300%. This trend has continued.

In 2006, it was reported that two-thirds of new UK businesses survive for at least two years, and 44% survive for at least four years.

Why was this? I was curious to understand why some succeeded whilst others failed.

These questions acted as a catalyst for the research into this area. More details of this research are outlined in **chapter 2. what the research said.**

This practical guide is a product of that research. It aims to help you to test the water and to see if self-employment is for you. If you decide that there is potential there, it aims to make it easier to transition into self-employment, irrespective of where you started. If you are already self-employed it can help you to provide a well needed personal business health check to kick start you and get you back on track. If you are already successfully self-employed and are wishing to start afresh with a new business idea, it will support you in that business start-up.

The guide aims to be accessible and practical. After these two introductory chapters, **chapters 3-10** walk through the eight factors that the research identified as being important to success. The factors are defined, then highlighted through case studies; you can develop your skills further through activities and exercises. Finally you consider your next steps through completing the personal planning section in **chapter 11. what does this mean for me?** and accessing other useful information in **chapter 12. where to get more help.**

Try to create a conducive, learning environment. This may involve creating some quiet time to read, work through and reflect. You are the best person to decide. Consider how you have learnt well in the past. What do you need to do to repeat this?

Before you start reading through, it might be useful for you to take stock and record your current thoughts and feelings about moving into self-employment. Use the questions below to help you take stock on your current position in relation to self-employment:

You can come back to this later on and see how these may have developed.

- What do you think about moving into self-employment?

- How do you feel about moving into self-employment?

- Using a score of 1 to 10, how much do you want to move into self-employment now: 1 being not at all, and 10 being absolutely?

- Using a score of 1 to 10, how ready are you to move into self-employment now: 1 being not at all, and 10 being absolutely?

- What unanswered questions do you have about moving into self-employment?

Enjoy this practical guide. I hope that it helps you to make choices and to potentially realise some of your dreams and ambitions.

[signature]

Cathy Brown

chapter 2. what the research said

This chapter provides more details about the research that this practical guide is based upon.

As part of my MSc, Occupational Psychology with Birkbeck, University of London, I had the chance to undertake some work-related research.

At the time, I too was making the transition to self-employment. All around me many friends, colleagues and acquaintances were also following a similar path. Some took the transition in their stride whilst others seemed to find it harder. This left me curious and wondering why this was so.

Looking at what made it easier to move to self-employment became the focus of the research.

Numerous people from around the UK took part in the research. What they had in common was that they:

- Had made the transition into self-employment within the last three years.

- Saw themselves as being successful in the transition.

- Agreed to have their stories shared in this guide to help others learn.

They came from a range of work areas including:

- Architecture
- Complementary therapies
- Creative design
- Energy development

- Human resources consultancy
- Landscape gardening
- Physiotherapy
- Translation

Eighteen months later, following the interview analysis, it became clear that:

8 factors accounted for 80% of the findings

In other words, 80% of what the participants described as being important to focus on to move successfully into self-employment can be defined by 8 factors.

Given this, it would follow that if we focus on building our capability in each of these eight factors, this may make a big difference in moving successfully into self-employment.

these eight factors can be clustered into three groups:

momentum for change

Push   Pull

1. restlessness with the current situation

2. passion for the work
3. clear vision

personal competencies

4. self management

5. self confidence

6. personal drive

physical support

7. financial buoyancy

8. advice sources

- Momentum for Change is all about having the impetus for the transition to self-employment. Is there enough of a push to move us from our current situation? Is there enough of a pull to move us towards self-employment?

- Personal Competencies relates to the personal behaviours and characteristics that helps us to move into self-employment. Do we have what it takes to move into self-employment? Are we up for developing ourselves?

- Physical Support relates to the practical arrangements that will help the transition. Do we have the practical considerations sorted out? What other useful arrangements do we need to make it easier to become self-employed?

Each of the eight factors will be explored in turn.

chapter 3. restlessness with the current situation

"I found it harder and harder on a daily basis to deal with the person at the top. He didn't delegate, and he didn't allow others to make a decision, so there was no chance of learning."

Simon, former IT programmer and now landscape gardener

This is the first of the eight factors that was seen as being useful in moving into self-employment. It is part of the first group, Momentum for Change.

What the research showed was that people who moved successfully into self-employment had a degree of restlessness with their current situation. In other words, they were experiencing a frustration with how things were right now, enough to get them motivated to want to change.

what this means is:

Feeling restless and unfulfilled with your current situation. This may relate to your work situation or life situation in general.

If you are restless with the current situation you are likely to think and experience some of the following:

- I have lost my way.
- I am doing my current work out of habit rather than enjoyment.
- I am not appreciated and valued in what I am doing.

bringing it alive: case study

Simon

Present Occupation - Landscape Gardener

Former Occupation - IT Programmer

In 1984 Simon joined a small IT consultancy in the Midlands. The company was set up by three directors and at the time he was their first employee. He joined as a computer programmer which was where his interest lay. *"I like the black and white aspect of programming – [you know what] works and doesn't work."*

In time as the company grew, the directors were keen for Simon to support its growth. They encouraged him to move into a management role. *"I was encouraged to go down the management route, despite saying that I didn't want to do that. In the end I was running a small team of programmers."*

Simon found it increasingly difficult working with the owners. He found that their style of management jarred with him. *"The head man who owned the company was Malaysian, he used to treat people like his family at home used to treat maids, 'do what I do, because I tell you to'."*

His frustrations and concerns all came to a head one day and Simon decided to leave. *"The time came where I couldn't really put up with it for any longer [...] it was like a volcano that builds up and builds up and gradually bulges and at some point it blows."*

Shortly after this Simon left the business. Initially he set up his own freelance IT consultancy. Over time both his confidence and ease at being self-employed grew. This enabled him to follow his true passion and he set up his own landscape gardening business.

a question

- How restless do you feel about your current work situation? Do you feel frustrated enough to want to change and make setting up your business happen?

building your capability

If you want to build your desire to change, here are some activities to build your capability in this area:

Activities

1. **This exercise will help you to find out the possible personal cost of not setting up a business.**
   Imagine yourself in 5 years time. Imagine that you didn't take the step to work out whether self-employment was for you. Consider the following questions:

- What would it be like for you to be still in your current situation, having made no progress?

- How would you feel explaining to family and friends that you once had a business idea but hadn't explored to see whether it was right for you?

- Take a few minutes to think about how you react to some of these questions. Does this change your desire at all to want to set up your own business?

2. **This exercise will help you to learn from others who have set up their own business.**
   Think of someone in your life who has recently set up their own business. Arrange to spend some time with them to find out what benefits they experience working for themselves.

- What questions could you ask to learn about what they get out of running their own business?

- When you are with them, notice how you react to them sharing their thoughts and benefits.

- Does hearing this change your desire to set up your own business?

3. **This exercise will help you to work out what helps you personally to change.**
Look back over your life so far and identify two or three times where you experienced change. This could be moving house, living abroad for a period of time, having a career change. Write these down.

- In each of these situations think about what caused you to change. Who initiated each change? Was it you or someone else? Was it something outside of your control?

- What do you notice about your responses? Are there any patterns?

- How might these observations help you in your transition to self-employment?

If you want to read more about creating this desire to change, here are some books that may help:

Books

- Chapters: creating a life of exhilaration and accomplishment in the face of change
  – Carpenter (2003) ISBN: 0071407928

- Change Dynamics For Creating Your Personal and Business Future – **R Grupe** (1994) ISBN: 0963249525

- Blueprint: Change your life from the inside out: understanding and controlling the invisible forces
  – creating your life – **Paul Drayton** (2003) ISBN: 1410795489

If you want additional resources to support your development within the area of personal change, here are some organisations that may be able to help you in this area:

Organisations that offer additional support

- www.businesslink.gov.uk

- www.excellencewithin.com

- www.alphaplustraining.com

chapter 4. passion for the work

"I'm passionate about reflexology, helping people and working with people [...] I don't mind putting my heart and soul into it because I love doing it. I feed it and it feeds me."

Rachel, former job centre manager and now reflexologist

This is the second of the eight factors that was seen as being useful in moving into self-employment. It is part of the first group, Momentum for Change.

What the research showed was that people who moved successfully into self-employment were totally passionate about their business idea. In other words, they were so excited about developing the business that they were compelled to want to take action and were driven to making their ideas and dreams a reality.

what this means is:

Feeling passionate and excited for your business idea.

This passion is found to be critical in helping you manage your own motivation and energy levels. If you are more passionate about what you do, you will find it easier to keep going when establishing your business.

In addition, it is found to be infectious; if you are passionate about your business, other people are more likely to support you in making your business a success.

Customers are also drawn towards exciting businesses. Your passion can win you business!

If you are passionate you are likely to think and experience some of the following:

- I can't stop talking about my business.
- I want to get on with it and make my business happen.
- Setting up my own business doesn't really seem like work.

© 2008 Evolve Consulting Services Limited

bringing it alive: case study

Rachel

Present Occupation - Reflexologist

Former Occupation - Job Centre Manager

In the 1990s Rachel worked as a manager in a job centre within Leicester. Whilst she enjoyed working there, she didn't feel fulfilled in what she did. She found ways of making it interesting. *"I did find a lot of it very repetitive and very boring. That's why I had to challenge myself to make it fun and interesting, as if we were achieving something."*

Whilst she took maternity leave, she had a chance to review her work situation. *"I was on maternity leave and enjoying spending time with my son when I realised that I actually didn't want to go back to work."*

Rachel began to develop her interest with reflexology and saw that this could be a new work opportunity. *"The more I looked at reflexology and found out about it, the more fascinated I became and I saw what it did and how it worked."*

"Originally I just wanted to do this for my family but I thought if I could do something to look after my family [...] perhaps I wouldn't have to go back to work. [...] perhaps I could take on a very mini sort of self-employed role."

Rachel took the step and decided to set up her own reflexology business. In her transition, the passion for her work grew. *"I felt as if someone had taken the lid off and I could fly [...] I was just so enthusiastic about it [...] watching people change when I worked with them was just so exhilarating. I wanted to do it more and more and more."*

She has come to learn that this passion for the business is important when moving into self-employment. *"If you're going to be self-employed you have to be passionate about it. [...] It's going to ask so much of you to make your business work that you've got to be prepared to put your heart and soul into it."*

Rachel now runs a very successful complementary therapy business. In 2004 she was nominated to be Business Woman of the Year 2005 by Leicestershire Chamber of Commerce.

a question

- How passionate are you about your business idea? How enthusiastic do you feel about translating your business idea into a reality?

building your capability

Here are some activities to build your passion for your work. Select those exercises that interest you the most, this may involve doing all three exercises:

Activities

1. **This exercise will help you to find out what energises you.**
    Look back over your life so far and identify the highs and lows. Pick out three to four high points where you enjoyed yourself and felt positive.

- What was it about these high points that made them so enjoyable? Describe these to a friend.

- Ask yourself, what themes do you notice?

- How could this inform your business idea?

2. **This exercise will help you to find out what types of work interests you.**
    Think about people in your life who are currently working. List down the nature of their work against their name. Once you have done this, look down the list and highlight those jobs or work areas that interest you.

- Which ones are you drawn towards?

- What attracts you to those jobs?

- How might this help you to identify what you enjoy?

3. **This exercise will help you to find out what you enjoy about life.**
   Gather together two to three friends to help you to brainstorm business ideas that you enjoy and feel energised about. Start off with a large plain sheet of paper. Write at the top of the page the activities that you enjoy in your life, for example: sailing, writing, keeping fit.

   • Using these as a starting point, brainstorm work ideas that are similar to these activities, for example: sailing instructor, journalist, personal trainer, working in PR, writing for a local magazine, school fitness instructor, etc.

   • Remember the rules of brainstorming: any ideas count, don't stop to discuss, the more ideas the better. Say the ideas out loud and write them on the paper.

   • Once you have the list, highlight those two to three ideas that you are drawn towards and decide on what small steps you will take to explore these business ideas.

If you want to read more about creating this passion for your business idea, here are some books that may help:

Books

• Love Your Job! **Paul Powers, Debby Russell** (1993) ISBN: 1565920368

• Love Your Job, Finding Your Passion: Work and the Spiritual Life **R M Kanter** (2000) ISBN: 0809139391

• Passion at Work: Six Secrets for Personal Success **Kevin Thomson** (1998) ISBN: 190096161X

If you want additional resources to support your development within the area of accessing what you are passionate about, here are some organisations that may be able to help you in this area:

Organisations that offer additional support

• www.canfieldcoaching.com

• www.heartatwork.net

• www.outlooktraining.org

chapter 5. clear vision

" I knew where I wanted to be [...] once I started to formulate ideas, the paths opened up and it evolved [...] it had many directions to go in and it kept changing."

**Suzanne, former employee of a physiotherapist practice
and now owner of a network of physiotherapy clinics**

This is the third of the eight factors that was seen as being useful in moving into self-employment. It is part of the first group, Momentum for Change.

What the research showed was that people who moved successfully into self-employment were clear about both the business proposition itself and what success meant for them personally. In other words, they knew what the business was going to offer, to which customer groups and to which geographical market, as well as what was important for them as individuals.

what this means is:

Being really clear about what the business is offering and the target customer groups.

Interestingly enough, the research findings highlighted that this clarity needed to be balanced with flexibility and the ability to 'go with the flow'. Often whilst the broad business proposition may have remained the same, the exact details may evolve and develop as experience grows.

In addition to clarifying the business proposition, it is found to be important to define what success is for you as a business owner. This may be different from the business definition of success. For example, this may mean that it is important to work three days per week, have two months off in the summer or work each day from 10am through to 3pm.

If you are clear about the vision you are likely to think and experience some of the following:

*   I describe my business idea quite freely to friends and answer their questions with confidence.

*   I spot opportunities to begin to convert my dream into a reality.

*   I know what a good year one looks like.

bringing it alive: case study

Suzanne

Present Occupation - Physiotherapy Clinic Owner

Former Occupation - Physiotherapist

In the late 1990s Suzanne worked as a physiotherapist within a practice aligned to a Doctor's surgery in South West London. Whilst she enjoyed her professional role, she felt undervalued by her employer and she knew that she could do a lot more. *"I was unhappy, I didn't feel like I was valued – I felt that I was capable of doing a lot more but no one was giving me the opportunity of doing that [...] I was working very hard behind the scenes but I wasn't getting anything back."*

This situation continued for some time until Suzanne came to realise that it wasn't sustainable and something had to change. *"I had put the effort in for three years and I didn't get anything back and so I stopped caring essentially for my job [...] I hit a dead end I think, so I knew that I had to move on [...] I felt that the only way to do it was to do it myself."*

Suzanne decided to bite the bullet and set up her own practice with a colleague of hers. They took time to develop the vision of the business and what they wanted to achieve. *"We kept on planning all the time, there was never a time when we didn't think about where we were at and where we wanted to be."*

They were clear about their business comprising a physiotherapy practice within Central London. However, they discovered that the finer details of this vision evolved as their experience grew. *"When we started we couldn't see the path but you could open doors and the path became very clear and we got swept up with that. The business took up a life of its own, the business led us rather than us lead it."*

"I knew where I wanted to be [...] once I started to formulate ideas, the paths opened up and it evolved [...] it had many directions to go in and it kept changing."

The ability to stay focused on the vision whilst going with the flow and allowing the business to evolve has enabled them to establish a successful physiotherapy practice. *"The business is thriving, it is growing and evolving still [...] it has exceeded our expectation and we are almost at the next stage of transition."*

"Because we have grown so fast, we are employing new staff, more reception cover, we have two more rooms in satellite locations, it has exploded."

Since being interviewed, the business has grown again. Suzanne and her business partner have extended their practice within Kensington and now employ six other physiotherapists. They have developed more clinic rooms and have extended the gymnasium.

a question

- How clear are you about your business proposition? What will business success look like for you personally?

building your capability

Here are some activities to build your vision for your business. Select those exercises that interest you the most, this may involve doing all three exercises:

Activities

1. **This exercise will help you to structure and develop your thinking in relation to your business proposition.**
   Take a sheet of paper and begin to sketch out your business proposition. Write down answers to the following questions:

- What are you offering – products and services? Who are your customers? Where are you working? What makes you different from other businesses in this field?

- With the help of a friend and taking no more than a couple of minutes, use the notes to describe your business proposition. Answer any questions that they may have.

- What impact has this had on the clarity of your business proposition?

2. **This exercise will help you to visualise your business and your personal definition of success.**
   Create a picture of your business proposition and your personal definition of success. In your picture, capture the products and services that you are offering, the customer profile and your location. Clarify what makes you different from your competitors. Clarify what success looks like for you personally. Use images and only use words sparingly.

- When you are happy with your picture, describe this picture to a friend and clarify what this picture means about your business proposition.

- Answer any questions that they may have.

- What difference has this made to your clarity of your vision?

3. **This exercise will help you to experience your business proposition.**
   Write down your ideal typical day when your business is up and running. Imagine yourself running your business. Write down step by step your perfect day. How does the day start? Who are you meeting? Where are you? What are you saying? What are you wearing? How are you feeling? What are you thinking?

- Once you have written this down, read this ideal typical day to a friend.

- What do you notice when you do this? What goes through your mind?

- How has this helped you clarify what success looks like for your business and yourself?

If you want to read more about creating clarity for your business idea, here are some books that may help:

Books

- Why didn't I Think of That Creativity in the Workplace **L Towe** (1996) ISBN 184926371

- Lateral Thinking for Management **E De Bono** (1990) ISBN 0140137807

- An Innovator's Tale **Craig Hickman** (2002) 0471-44388-3

If you want additional resources to support your development within the area of developing your visioning ability, here are some organisations that may be able to help you in this area:

Organisations that offer additional support

- www.mindstore.com
- www.leadershipconnections.co.uk
- www.qopd.co.uk

chapter 6. self management

"Over time I've been more conscious and I have more consciously chosen whom I spend time with and who I don't. It is especially helpful in terms of managing my energies. It is important to create an environment that supports what I do, that is very important to me."

**Nicola, former employee of a management consultancy
and now owner of a Human Resource consultancy**

This is the fourth of the eight factors that was seen as being useful in moving into self-employment. It is part of the second group, Personal Competencies.

What the research showed was that people who moved successfully into self-employment were self aware and were able to manage themselves in different situations. In other words, they knew what makes them tick, and they knew what to do to stay motivated and have a positive view of their business.

what this means is:

Having a clear understanding of your own preferences, strengths and development areas.

In a sense, it is about understanding what makes you unique. For example, do you like having a lot of people around, or do you prefer your own space? Are you strong in using numbers, or are you an ideas person?

In addition to understanding yourself, self management involves knowing what to do to set yourself up for success. It is about making decisions to allow you to perform to your best. For example, if you work best around other people, on days where you are due to work alone, you may arrange to see a friend for lunch so that you keep your energy and motivation up.

If you are effective at self management you are likely to think and experience some of the following:

- I do practical things that help me stay on top form in the work place.
- I know where my strengths lie and realise when I need external support for areas that are outside of my expertise.
- I am energised about the business.

bringing it alive: case study

Nicola

Present Occupation - Human Resource Consutancy Owner

Former Occupation - Senior Management Consultant

In early 2000, Nicola worked as a senior consultant within an international management consultancy within London. She focused on developing senior leaders and had played a role in the design of an on-line development product for leaders. Invited to join the team responsible for the product, she felt disappointed when her new job failed to materialise. *"They had always been terribly grateful for my contribution and credited me with making a significant contribution to the set up of [the team's core product]."*

"I had agreed to join that team and perform a particular role [...] so I joined the team, and one week later [...], the team manager announced that he was leaving. The team fell into disarray, [...] and my job just didn't materialise."

Nicola decided to use this as an opportunity to leave and to establish her own business. This would allow her to continue to make the difference in education in a way that was important to her. *"The reason why I made the move is because I wanted to be involved in education [...] I wanted to make a difference to the whole system and realising that if I actually became independently employed, I had scope to explore what that contribution might look like over time, whilst earning."*

Despite this clarity of vision, this transition to self-employment was scary for her. Nicola was very aware of her feelings. *"Right from the beginning I was afraid of the finances [...], I was operating out of fear and anxiety being out of work. If you translate that to being with a client and in a sales situation, that is not a good place to be in terms of selling, and it has all sorts of implications, [...] you may say yes to work that you really don't want."*

Given this, Nicola took steps to manage her anxieties. She signed up for a NLP practitioner course. This gave her a lot of confidence and strength. *"Before I made the decision to leave [...] I had been thinking about NLP (neuro-linguistic programming), and I had been having some discussions with my friends about NLP. I had started to look at providers and think about it, when I decided to leave [...] that became really urgent for two main reasons. One was that I didn't want to feel that I was a freelance consultant doing [the same] things, so actually experiencing this different technology was part of becoming me with a kit bag of skills [...], and secondly I was s**t scared!"*

"So there was something about doing it at that time, [...] in the early months it provided a magical experience in itself and also it provided a support."

As well as doing the course, Nicola got to see that some people helped her in her transition to self-employment and some people got in the way. She used these insights to decide who to spend time with. *"I am thinking about relationships, on the one hand there were a whole range of relationships who really helped me during that period, there were also a whole load of people who didn't!"*

"So there were plenty of doubters and I suppose again the thing for me was to be noticing the relationships that were helping me and making decisions of how to handle those conversations that could really drag me down."

"Over time I've been more conscious and I have more consciously chosen whom I spend time with and who I don't. It is especially helpful in terms of managing my energies. It is important to create an environment that supports what I do, that is very important to me."

Nicola is now into her fourth year of running her Human Resource consultancy in London. During that time she has continued to nurture her own development, to refine her vision and to take steps to bring her vision to fruition. She continues to work with clients in business to develop leadership at senior levels. At the same time, she has built a portfolio of activities designed to promote and develop effective leadership in schools.

a question

- How well do you know yourself and what makes you tick? What can you do to increase your energy levels?

building your capability

Here are some activities to build your self management skills. Select those exercises that interest you the most, this may involve doing all three exercises:

Activities

1. **This exercise will help you clarify your strengths and work out when you are on top form.**
   Take a sheet of paper and identify four to six situations when you have felt that you have performed to the best of your ability. Think about what led this to be the case.

   - Was it because you were using particular strengths? If so, describe these. Was it down to the situation that you were in? Did the people around you make a difference?

   - Identify the ingredients of what led you to be on top form and write these down.

   - Consider how you can use these insights to set yourself up for being a success in self-employment.

2. **This exercise will help you to manage your energy levels.**
   Again, take some paper and reflect back over the last two to three months. Identify the occasions when you felt happy and full of energy. As they occur to you, write these down. They can be at any time during the day, irrespective of whether they occurred during work or outside of work.

   - Was it when you were doing a particular sport? Was it when you were with friends?

   - Did you find that it was when you had time to yourself to recharge your batteries?

   - Once you are confident that you have a good short list, ask yourself how you can weave these activities into your life when you are self employed.

3. This exercise will help you to learn from others in this area.
Identify two to three people in your life who run their own business and who you feel you can talk to about your ideas of setting up your own business. Arrange to spend some time with them. Take time to understand how they keep motivated and keep going.

- What is it that they do to keep their energies high? How do they keep motivated, even when they have had a challenging day? What is it that they do? Who do they see?

- When you listen to their answers, notice how you respond. Which ideas appeal to you?

- How could you learn from their experiences?

If you want to read more about building your self awareness and self management, here are some books that may help:

Books

- The Celestine Vision: Living the New Spiritual Awareness **James Redfield** (1997) ISBN 0446675237

- The Seven Habits of Highly Effective People **S R Covey** (1987) ISBN 0684858398

- Feel the Fear and Do it Anyway **S Jeffers** (1995) ISBN 0712671056

If you want additional resources to support your development within the area of self awareness and self management, here are some organisations that may be able to help you in this area:

Organisations that offer additional support

- www.TalentSmart.com

- www.eiworld.org

- www.EISGlobal.com

chapter 7. self confidence

"Financially can we afford to do what we are doing? I have a belief and trust that we are doing the right thing [...] it is constantly believing that we can do this. We can be successful."

**Tony, former business developer of a design consultancy
and now co-owner of a design consultancy**

This is the fifth of the eight factors that was seen as being useful in moving into self-employment. It is part of the second group, Personal Competencies.

What the research showed was that people who moved successfully into self-employment believed in themselves and were confident in their own capability. In other words, they knew they had it in them to do well and they had a positive outlook for the business.

what this means is:

Believing in yourself, in your capability and your ability to make things happen.

In essence, it is about knowing that you can make it a success, whatever happens.

In addition it is about having a positive view of the future. Despite the set backs and the ups and downs of setting up a business, it is about believing it will all come through in the end and be successful.

If you are self confident you are likely to think and experience some of the following:

*   I believe I can make it a success.
*   I can see the value of my personal skills and experiences.
*   I know the business is going to work out and I have a positive outlook on the future.

bringing it alive: case study

Tony

Present Occupation - Design Consultancy Co-owner

Former Occupation - Business Developer

In 2004, Tony worked as a business developer in a design consultancy within Nottingham. Whilst he had suffered from ill health for a number of years, recently he had begun to experience some pressure to leave the business. *"I was diagnosed with Crohn's disease about 6 years ago and this has effected how a lot of people perceive me now. Employers tend to see me as an ill person, and their perception had changed. I was a very successful sales person [...] I was top in the company [...] they tried to put pressure on me the time that I was taken sick. This added pressure, so that I had to go in when I wasn't feeling well."*

This led him to begin to rethink his work-life balance, and he started to explore the option of going into partnership with a colleague and establishing their own design consultancy. *"So I was thinking that the only way to do this was to go self-employed working with a business partner, finding something that fitted with my life style and ideals. [...] The opportunity came out to work with [Mark] and we sat down and thought about it."*

Tony took the plunge and left his job. Initially he found the transition challenging. *"So yes – I resigned. Then I realised that I had no money – and it was worrying."*

However, this was where his self belief began to help him through these challenging times. *"Financially can we afford to do what we are doing? I have a belief and trust that we are doing the right thing [...] it is constantly believing that we can do this. We can be successful."*

"We have a belief in each other, so most things can be tackled between the two of us – and it is not taking things on that you can't do. It is working to each of our strengths, and, if we don't have something, then we ask someone who has. You create this 'you can't fail' mentality – and it is a belief."

In addition, Tony's belief in his own ability supported him as well. *"Being a salesman is the only skill that I have got, I have been very successful in sales and have bought in £1million orders!"*

The business has gone from strength to strength, they have had to consider whether to start employing other people.

They are now into their third year of running their design consultancy in the East Midlands. They are expanding and have had to move to larger premises where they now employ a team of seven to help the business to continue to grow.

a question

- Do you believe in yourself? Are you confident in your own abilities? How do you feel about the future of your business?

building your capability

Here are some activities to build your self confidence. Select those exercises that interest you the most, this may involve doing all three exercises:

Activities

1. **This exercise will help you to identify and change those beliefs that get in the way.**
   What we believe to be true affects what we do and therefore the results that we can achieve.

For example, if we believe that we are useless at making presentations, we are likely to feel uneasy and unsure and this may lead us to present in a tentative and uncertain manner. Alternatively, if we believe that we are capable at making presentations, we are likely to feel comfortable and this may lead us to come across as confident and natural whilst presenting.

- Take some time to identify those beliefs that potentially may get in the way for your moving to self-employment.

- For these beliefs consider an alternative that is more positive.

- Focus on these new beliefs at the beginning of each day. Start to look for evidence to back up these new beliefs.

2. **This exercise will help you to build your self confidence.**
   Identify five to six people who know you well and who you trust and respect. Ask them if they are interested in supporting you in your transition to self-employment. Arrange to spend some time with them, and ask them for feedback on when they have seen you at your best. Get specifics from them. Ask them for the details of the occasions. Clarify what you did, what you said that made them see you at your best.

   - Once you have this feedback from everyone, what do you notice when you look at what people said?

   - Identify the patterns across the feedback. What are the similarities?

   - How can you incorporate this into your plans for moving to self-employment? How can you create more situations where you are at your best?

3. **This exercise will help you to become more positive in your thinking.**
   What we know is whatever we choose to focus on gets larger in proportion. For example, if we focus on problems, we will see more problems and they will take up a larger part of the day. If we choose to focus on positives, then we will see more positive situations and they will become the larger part of our day.

   - Buy yourself a notebook, make sure it is of a size convenient for easy access and use. For the next week, record daily anything positive you have done, been pleased with, has happened to you, possible business leads etc.

   - At the end of each day highlight those positives that are interesting and worth thinking more about.

   - At the end of the week, notice and write down the themes that are emerging. Consider how this might be useful in your transition to self-employment.

If you want to read more about building your self confidence, here are some books that may help:

Books

- I'm OK, You're OK **T Harris** (1995) ISBN 0099552418
- Learned Optimism **M E Pseligram** (1998) ISBN 0671019112
- How to Stop Worrying & Start Living **D Carnegie** (1990) ISBN 0749307234

If you want additional resources to support your development within the area of self confidence, here are some organisations that may be able to help you in this area:

Organisations that offer additional support

- www.itsnlp.com
- www.excellencewithin.com
- www.reedlearning.co.uk

chapter 8. personal drive

"I would say that the quality of what you do should be an absolute priority [...] I have run my management programme, I am continuously improving it. I am wanting to do it better."

**Margaret, former training and development consultant
and now owner of a training and development consultancy**

This is the sixth of the eight factors that was seen as being useful in moving into self-employment. It is part of the second group, Personal Competencies.

What the research showed was that people who moved successfully into self-employment were:

- Focused on continually improving what they did and learning how things could be better.

- Resilient when the going gets tough.

- Personally driven to keep going at all times.

what this means is:

Being focused on improving everything about the business at all times.

This could mean all sorts of things including looking at the products and services being offered, the administration processes being used, the marketing approach, etc.

In addition it is about picking yourself up after challenging times, being determined to win through and having the tenacity to keep going when you may feel like giving up.

If you have high personal drive you are likely to think and experience some of the following:

- I ask myself how I can do what I do better.

- I ask for feedback from my customers to help me to improve.

- I get back to work when I feel fed up or let down by some disappointing news.

bringing it alive: case study

Margaret

Present Occupation - Training & Development Consultancy Owner

Former Occupation - Training & Development Consultant

Margaret worked as a training and development consultant with a leading health and beauty retailer. She focused on management development and leadership coaching and she enjoyed what she did. However, in the early 2000s there was a change of focus in the work, which didn't make sense to her. *"The goal posts had changed, the new work was very unexciting and very uninteresting, it seemed to be wanting different skills from me which I didn't think that I possessed. So I went from a hands on coach and facilitator, to a project manager. All of a sudden they didn't want the skills that I had, and they wanted a project manager."*

"It almost felt like they had taken away the important work and gave us something that was less important. So we went from focusing on senior managers and the retail teams – the regional retail teams – to focusing on human resource development and it didn't seem right."

This change of focus frustrated Margaret and led her to consider her options. *"I needed to do work that I felt was making a difference, that I was proud of and that I found energizing, and it just wasn't happening."*

The offer of redundancies made it easier for Margaret to leave. It allowed her to consider going self-employed. *"I think that it would be interesting to see if the redundancy hadn't have come up, would I have jumped ship or would I have hung on? I don't know the answer to that question. [...] I have thought of working for myself and yes, they are paying me to leave. That was the icing on the cake. I don't know if I would have been brave enough to leave if I didn't have that cushion of that payment, I don't know."*

Margaret had decided to take some time out before starting work. However a work opportunity came through ahead of time. *"I really decided that I would take a few months off. So my intention was leaving [company name], and then taking some time off for the rest of the year [...] I got a phone call from someone to say 'would you do this piece of work?'."*

"The first piece of work that I did was for another consultant. I have not felt so nervous for a long time."

This initial nervousness led Margaret to realise the importance of delivering good quality work. *"All of a sudden I had been asked to do a piece of work that I was paid for. I was an independent consultant and that was a completely different mind set to have. If I don't do this well, I am letting myself down, I am going to let my consultant down who employed me, I am going to be letting the people down and I felt really wound up about it."*

In time Margaret came to see the importance of continually improving her work in her business. *"I think that the only thing that keeps occurring every now and then, is when I say to myself 'ok, when is my next piece of work coming from?'."*

"I have probably over prepared for my work, and it has been important for me to deliver top class material. Inevitably, when I have completed a contract, the easy way of getting new work is through those contacts."

Margaret has learnt that this drive for continual improvement has enabled her to win additional business. *"My husband thinks that I over prepare, but because I have delivered some really good stuff and I get referrals from that piece of work, I would say that the quality of what you do should be an absolute priority - to be the best."*

"Whenever I rerun my management courses I am continuously improving them. I am wanting to do it better each time I run them."

Margaret continues to run her Training and Development Consultancy in the Midlands, and deliver outstanding work with an established client base.

- How could you improve your products and services? How important is it for you to succeed? How much drive do you have to keep going even when the going gets tough?

building your capability

Here are some activities to build your personal drive and determination. Select those exercises that interest you the most, this may involve doing all three exercises:

Activities

1. **This exercise will help you to find out what is important to your potential clients.**
   Identify three to four of your potential clients who you would be interested in approaching for feedback.

- Arrange to spend some time with them to understand what would be important to them if they were to purchase the products or services you are planning to sell as part of your business.

- Plan the questions that you will ask in the interview. These questions could include: what is important for you when purchasing x?, what irritates you currently when purchasing x?, etc.

- Use the interview findings to enhance your business offer.

2. **This exercise will help you to build your personal drive.**
   Identify three to four people who know you well and who you would describe as personally-driven, focused and tenacious. Approach them to arrange a conversation with them to understand what it is that they do which contributes to their drive and focus.

- Create a list of questions for your conversation. These questions could include: what leads you to be so driven? What enables you to keep going even in situations where you feel disappointed? What compels you to keep improving what you do in your business?, etc.

- Listen to what is said and notice what occurs to you.

- Consider how you can learn from their techniques and insights to facilitate your move into self-employment.

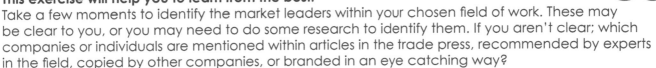

3. **This exercise will help you to learn from the best.**
Take a few moments to identify the market leaders within your chosen field of work. These may be clear to you, or you may need to do some research to identify them. If you aren't clear; which companies or individuals are mentioned within articles in the trade press, recommended by experts in the field, copied by other companies, or branded in an eye catching way?

- Once you have your two to three market leaders, now is your chance to learn from them. Find out their ingredients for success. The more specific you can be the better.

- You could act as an enquiring customer and experience their service first hand; you could ask for information. Find out what makes them the best.

- Consider how can you match or exceed these market leaders for your customers.

If you want to read more about building your personal drive, here are some books that may help:

Books

- A Passion for Excellence **T Peters & Nancy Austin** (1986) ISBN 0006370624

- The Goal **E Goldratt** (1986) ISBN 056607184

- Biographies of High Achievers e.g. **L Iacocca, R Branson, C Bonnington**

If you want additional resources to support your development within the area of personal drive, here are some organisations that may be able to help you in this area:

Organisations that offer additional support

- www.excellencewithin.com

- www.alphaplustraining.com

- www.mindstore.com

chapter 9. financial buoyancy

"I had a huge security driver, so I needed to make sure that I took care of that. What made that possible was this chunk of money behind me, and what made it possible was this severance."

**Fiona, former human resource professional
and now owner of a human resource consultancy**

This is the seventh of the eight factors that was seen as being useful in moving into self-employment. It is part of the third group, Physical Support.

What the research showed was that people who moved successfully into self-employment had plans in place to guarantee some form of a positive cash flow or income stream during their initial transitional period. This practical arrangement was achieved through a variety of means.

what this means is:

Having the security of a positive cash flow during the first few months of self-employment.

This could be achieved through a range of means. For some this may involve using savings, and for others this may involve using a redundancy payment. Others may involve receiving physical financial support via a partner, and for others it may mean getting a part-time job.

To help to retain some continuity during the transition, some people mirror the idea of being employed through paying themselves a salary each month from their financial source.

The research highlighted that a general rule of thumb was that people felt that they need a financial lump sum that covered six months of living expenses.

If you have high financial buoyancy you are likely to think and experience some of the following:

* I feel financially secure for the short term (up to six months).
* I am confident that I can maintain my standard of living during the transition.
* I have set up a new cash flow arrangement where income is received regularly through a defined financial source.

bringing it alive: case study

Fiona

Present Occupation - Human Resource Consultancy Owner

Former Occupation - Human Resource Professional

Fiona worked as a Head of Learning and Development with a well-known consumer organisation in the East Midlands. Her role focused on developing the capabilities of head office personnel. She had been toying with the idea of going self-employed for 5 years. Under a head office restructure programme in 2003, the opportunity came up for some people to take voluntary redundancy. "[The CEO] made an announcement that he would like to make 800 redundancies, and he sparked a conversation that I had been having over the last five years where I had flirted with going into self-employment, and working outside of [the business] – I hadn't had the courage to do it and the circumstances hadn't been right before."

This redundancy opportunity provided an opportunity for Fiona. "In some ways this lent itself to perpetuating my dream [...] to have the courage to do something that wasn't connected to an organisation and to go solo."

Although this move to self-employment was a big step for Fiona, she decided to take the plunge. "I had flirted with it for 5 years, what I couldn't figure out was 'was I good enough?'"

"Then I decided that I should seize life and should grab it by the scruff of the neck and just go for it. So that is what I did."

However at home Fiona was responsible for paying the mortgage. This financial commitment was an issue for her. The decision to go self-employed wasn't taken lightly. "I was thinking 'do it girl!', but we have a huge mortgage, and so it was like, god – I have got to keep doing this [...] if I fail at this, I take my whole family down – mortgage and everything."

Given this financial responsibility Fiona took steps to put some practical plans in place to provide financial buoyancy. "I had a huge security driver, so I needed to make sure that I took care of that. What made that possible was this chunk of money behind me, and what made it possible was this severance."

"I took it and put it in a bank account and I paid myself the same salary that I would normally receive [...] That has given me the security blanket I need and I know that from what I have in that account and what I have been paid in the business, I have one years' salary of what I would normally have."

"I need to make sure that the next 6 months are cared for and so I don't worry about them and don't feel threatened and pushed to the wall."

When Fiona was asked what advice she would give to people who were thinking about going self-employed, she said "Go with it – and put some contingencies behind you – like mine is teaching, but I also know that if I need to go and get a job I can go and find one tomorrow. You have got to believe in yourself and you need contingencies – and if you don't have those contingencies – then put them in place, because you don't look back."

This severance payment gave her financial buoyancy and made it possible to move into self-employment. "I had been toying with doing my business, and I just saw the opportunity. Taking redundancy made it more attractive, by putting £Xk in the bank, I thought, hey there is my salary, whereas before I needed the security. It is my role to pay the mortgage, I had taken care of my responsibility to our household and so I had this freedom."

Fiona's business goes from strength to strength. She is active in helping individuals and businesses flourish.

- How could you guarantee a positive cash flow? What income do you need to sustain your standard of living during your transition to self-employment?

building your capability

Here are some activities to build your financial buoyancy. Select those exercises that interest you the most, this may involve doing all three exercises:

Activities

1. **This exercise will help you to understand your financial requirements.**
   Either take a sheet of paper or open up a spreadsheet. Make a list of your living expenses over the course of a typical month. You may want to refer to your bank statement or receipts over the course of the last two to three months for information. Some of the expenses will be exact and predictable, for example tax disc for car, whilst others may be more variable, for example food bill. Make assumptions where the costs are variable.

- Having done this, highlight those that are essential and those that are desirable. Add up these monthly living expenses. You will be able to calculate your essential living expense total, and your desirable living expense total. This will give you a clear indication of what cash flow requirements you have in your transition.

- What financial buoyancy do you need to manage for the first six months of self-employment?

- How may you meet this financial requirement?

2. **This exercise will help you to find out potential, part-time income sources to supplement your transition to self-employment.**
   Write down a list of your own skills and experiences. Once you are happy with this list, take a piece of plain paper and create as many ideas as possible that use these skills and experiences to generate income. Write down all ideas, however unusual they may seem. Enrol the support of a friend if you think this will make it more fruitful.

- Once you have run out of ideas, sit back and look at the list.

- Which ones are you drawn towards? Which ones interest you?

- Identify two or three of the ideas that you are willing to explore to see how they can increase your financial buoyancy.

3. This exercise will help you to learn from others.
Identify two or three people who you know who have moved into self-employment within the last couple of years. See if they are happy to spend some time with you to support you in your move to self-employment.

- Ahead of meeting them, generate some questions to identify what they did to support their financial buoyancy. Aim to get as many tips as possible to help you with your practical plans to build your own financial buoyancy.

- During the meeting, write down their ideas and insights. Notice which ones stand out to you.

- Which ideas are useful for you to build your financial buoyancy?

If you want to read more about building your financial buoyancy, here are some books that may help:

Books

- The Tricks of the Rich: what they don't want you to know about making money and accumulating wealth – **Paul A Overy and Ken Lee** (2006) ISBN 1904887090

- Winning the Cash Flow War: your ultimate survival guide to making money and keeping it – **Fred Rewey** (2005) ISBN 0471711535

- The ABCs of Making Money: painless strategies for ordinary people to create extraordinary wealth – **Denis Cauvier** (2003) ISBN 013047486X

If you want additional resources to support your development within the area of financial buoyancy, here are some organisations that may be able to help you in this area:

Organisations that offer additional support

- www.learndirect.co.uk

- www.businesslink.gov.uk

- www.icslearn.co.uk

This guide on financial buoyancy is produced for general guidance only. Cathy Brown does not offer financial advice. If you require such advice then, I urge you to seek the opinion of an appropriate professional.

chapter 10. advice sources

"Mentally it is exhausting, it is endless, day after day you are meeting people, and you need positive reinforcement. It may even be bouncing ideas off someone, 'this is something I am starting to get a sense of, or do you think that I should be working with this type of company, or attract this sort of ...', so it is a sounding board."

Millie, former consultant and now business coach

This is the eighth and final factor that was seen as being useful in moving into self-employment. It is part of the third group, Physical Support.

What the research showed was that people who moved successfully into self-employment had a well-established network of friends, colleagues and acquaintances. This network of contacts provided a useful source of advice in the transition to self-employment.

what this means is:

Having a well-established group of contacts that can provide different types of support at different times, helping you move into self-employment.

The research showed that people needed three types of support:

- Practical support – this is made up of physical, practical support that is required on occasions when running a business. This may include child-care support, picking up the children from school on particular days. It also may comprise support with household chores and responsibilities.

- Technical support – this is expert advice in areas outside of your own capability. For some this may include help with setting up a computer or deciding whether to be a sole trader versus a limited business. For others it may include legal advice on contracts, or how to negotiate a price.

- Emotional support – this is support from people close to you, who can help you through the more challenging times. These are the people who will be there to help you work through a difficult situation, and help you to bounce back after a set back.

If you have a well-established network of advice sources you are likely to think and experience some of the following:

- I already talk and discuss with my friends about the business and the transition to self-employment.

- I work out the practical support needed to help in certain situations when being self-employed.

- I ask around for recommended providers of IT, finance, legal support etc.

bringing it alive

Let's now elaborate on this by looking at three mini case studies from the research addressing the areas of practical, technical and emotional support.

case study 1: practical support

Richard

Present Occupation - Energy Specialist

Former Occupation - Management Consultant

Richard was working as a consultant for an international management consultancy on a part-time basis. He was juggling a range of professional commitments, and a bout of ill health encouraged him to make a choice and follow his passions of setting up an energy specialist firm.

Richard was working 90% of his time with an international management consultancy which took him to different parts of the world. The remaining half a day each week provided him with an opportunity to juggle other interests and commitments. *"I was working for a consulting group 90% of my time. As well as this, I was trustee for two charities, unpaid, and I had started the [energy] project in December of 2002, so I had a number of external interests […] I ended up with all of my commitments in March 2003, I had 26 projects."*

This heavy work commitment led to a bout of illness. This encouraged Richard to make a choice. *"I was utterly and totally ill, I have never been ill in my life. I had pneumonia, six to eight weeks in the Spring. I was going into work on Monday and Tuesday and being knocked out on Wednesday and being ill and kind of just about recovering by Friday and by Monday I was OK again."*

"I thought, this is crazy, you need to do one thing, you have to choose now, and so I went back and said that I have made a decision."

Richard left the international consultancy and decided to take the plunge and set up his own energy specialist business. *"There was a relief that I got rid of 22 of my 26 initiatives."*

Building up this energy specialist business from home required physical support from his wife and family. *"Well I think domestic support is important, and the relationship between work and family life is very different from when you are in employment, because an organization has very clear boundaries, so it is very acceptable to say I am sorry I am late home because something has cropped up."*

"Whereas if you say 'I can't make it for supper – I will stay in my office until midnight', that is perceived to be different. And I can feel very guilty."

Richard has found it challenging at times managing the physical boundaries between work and family commitments. This has led him to set up a clear working agreement with his wife. *"I have had bad times personally when I have been wanting to separate things more and emails have been coming in and on Sunday night – I wanted to view them."*

"We have a very firm working structure at the moment, it is quite stable, I never work on Saturday, so Saturday is a clear family day and I always work on Sunday morning when Jane takes the children to church."

This working agreement is particularly important for Richard. Setting up a research-based business takes time and requires family support and understanding. *"Because the work is long term, I am not getting the money coming in. It is more research based, and that can be tough because you have no money coming in for weeks, and yet we are saying that I can't pick the children up from school. […] I am very lucky because my wife is very supportive."*

Richard's long-term development is paying off. The business is now generating a healthy income. It employs 12 people and is run out of two offices.

case study 2: technical support

Craig

Present Occupation - Occupational Psychology Consultancy Owner

Former Occupation - Assistant Clinical Psychologist

Craig was working in the NHS as an assistant clinical psychologist. Whilst psychology was an area of interest, he felt undervalued by his line manager. This gave him the impetus to set up his occupational psychology consultancy. *"I did feel very devalued and frustrated, it probably speeded up my desire to leave."*

"They re-advertised my post without telling me. I told my line manager that I was shocked to see my job advertised, to which she replied that she thought that I was interested in this occupational thing. That for me was a message saying that I was clearly not wanted by my department."

This gave Craig the motivation to consider developing his own business. From having worked in the NHS, he felt that this was a big step for him. *"The brave new world comes to mind, completely unknown, something new and without boundaries, which with my kind of personality does make me slightly anxious. It's like starting a journey which you don't know where it will end."*

Asking for technical and professional advice helped him with the transition into running his own consultancy. *"I think for me the greatest help has been the professional business advisor, [they] can tell you how things are done because they have done it themselves."*

"I think of those people going in to self-employment but not going to the seminars and making those connections were very disadvantaged. Certainly for me going through that transition and meeting the advisor, I then had someone who I could bounce ideas off and I could be quite realistic and so, on a practical sense, that helped me a lot. Finding out what it means to be self-employed is very important."

"I tell people that it is the best thing that I have done, career wise."

Craig now runs a successful occupational psychology consultancy where he works with individuals and organisations in the areas of stress management, communication and assertiveness.

case study 3: emotional support

Millie

Present Occupation - Coaching Business Owner

Former Occupation - Human Resource Consultant

Millie worked as a consultant within an international human resources consultancy. She was based in London, although she originated from Australia. She was dissatisfied with her work situation and had always dreamt of setting up her own coaching business. During 2002 she was offered redundancy; she decided to take the step and set up her own business.

Whilst Mille worked at the consultancy in London, she was expected to work across a broad range of areas. This didn't work for her. She wanted to be able to focus on developing her coaching skills. *"I felt very unsupported, 'Can you do this? Can you do that?' – it was like jack of all trades and master of none. I wasn't enjoying the nature of the work; I wasn't enjoying the inability to specialise."*

The redundancy offer came as a perfect opportunity for Millie to set up her own coaching business. *"Being made redundant gave me this opportunity, it was given to me on a beautiful silver plate!"*

However, despite this financial support, Mille found the transition to self-employment challenging. *"It was very scary, you are on your own. You are not getting that much feedback, you need to get work – it is not just fun and games. Business needs to happen."*

She became very clear about the support that she needed from her husband. *"I needed partner backing [...] to do it on your own is a real hurdle, in every way, financially, mentally and emotionally. To have someone supporting you in all of those ways is really important."*

When Millie was asked to describe this emotional support in more detail, here is her response. *"Mentally it is exhausting, it is endless, day after day you are meeting people, and you need positive reinforcement. It may even be bouncing ideas off someone, 'this is something I am starting to get a sense of, or do you think that I should be working with this type of company, or attract this sort of ...', so it is a sounding board to things that were happening in my mind."*

"I came from Australia so I am in a country where I am meeting a lot of people who are a different culture to me, so that was more exhausting, rather than being in Australia or being on my own. So for me it was tough."

Since being interviewed, Millie has moved back to Australia with her husband and children. Her coaching business continues to flourish within the Sydney area.

a question

- How extensive is your network of contacts? Who in your life could provide you with your practical, technical and emotional support that you need?

building your capability

Here are some activities to build your advice sources. Select those exercises that interest you the most, this may involve doing all three exercises:

Activities

1. **This exercise will help you to understand and meet your needs for practical support and technical support.**
   Create a table on a piece of paper or a spreadsheet. Draw two columns and label one practical support and the other technical support.

- Brainstorm under each column the types of support that you believe that you need or will need when you move into self-employment. For example, under practical support this may include: child care cover, cooking, shopping etc. Under technical support this may include: accountancy, legal, IT, web design, brand design etc.

- Once you are happy that you have got the main headings, then access your contact list and begin to put the names of people that you know against these support areas.

- Where you have gaps, consider who do you know that may know someone who can help in this area.

2. **This exercise will help you to identify those people who can provide emotional support in your transition to self-employment.**
   Think about the times over the last two to three years where you have needed someone to talk to, perhaps work through a particular issue. Who were the people that were there for you then?

- Consider who in your life you enjoy spending time with, and who leaves you feeling energised and more positive? Who do you know that really understands you and listens to you?

- Look at the list of people who come to mind when you consider these questions.

- Consider which people could support you now when you may need them.

3. This exercise will help you to learn from others.
Identify two to three people who you know who have moved into self-employment within the last couple of years. See if they are happy to spend some time with you to support you in your move to self-employment.

- Ahead of meeting them, generate some questions to identify what support they needed to make the transition. This may be practical, technical and emotional support. Consider your own support needs, are there any gaps in your network list?

- During the meeting, write down their advice sources. Fill any gaps that you may have.

- Notice which ones stand out to you. Which sources are useful for you to build your advice network?

If you want to read more about building your network of advice sources, here are some books that may help:

Books

- It's Who You Know: career strategies for making effective personal contacts
  – **Cynthia Chin-Lee** (1996) ISBN -10: 0893842230

- Networking for Success: The Art of Establishing Personal Contacts
  – **Nancy Flynn** (2003) ISBN –10: 1560526823

- Confident Networking For Career Success and Satisfaction
  – **Gael Lindenfield and Stuart Lindenfield** (2005) ISBN – 10: 0749926503

If you want additional resources to support your development within the area of developing your networks, here are some organisations that may be able to help you in this area:

Organisations that offer additional support

- www.learndirect.co.uk
- www.businesslink.gov.uk
- www.icslearn.co.uk

chapter 11. what does this mean for me?

Now that we have walked through each of the eight factors, this is a natural time to pause and consider 'what this means for me'.

In **chapter 1. setting the scene** you were invited to spend some time to reflect upon how you felt and what you thought about moving into self-employment at that time. Some questions were posed to help you to do this. Let's take stock and see how this has potentially developed.

taking stock

Create a comfortable environment for you to reflect and take stock on your position in relation to self-employment. You may choose to do this on your own, or to talk it through with a friend or colleague.

The questions below may help you do this:

_____

• Which of the eight factors do you think are your strengths?

_____

• Which of the eight factors do you think would require some development?

_____

• What do you now think about moving into self-employment?

- How do you now feel about moving into self-employment?

- Using a score of 1 to 10, how much do you want to move into self-employment now: 1 being not at all, and 10 being absolutely?

- Using a score of 1 to 10, how ready are you to move into self-employment now: 1 being not at all, and 10 being absolutely?

- What do you notice about how these answers compare against your initial answers from Chapter 1?

You may be in a number of different places. Let's work through each of these scenarios in turn.

'No thank you!'

Reading through this practical guide and answering the questions for yourself may have led you to decide that self-employment is definitely not for you.

It may have confirmed the risks of moving into self-employment. It may have clarified the benefits of being employed as opposed to being self-employed. It may have highlighted the impracticalities of you being self-employed.

Either way, whatever the reasons, making a clear choice not to move into self-employment can be seen as a positive outcome. So well done in working through your thinking and coming to that conclusion.

'I'm still not sure'

Working through this practical guide may have answered some questions but may have also generated some other questions. This may have left you thinking, I'm still not sure whether self-employment is for me.

If this is the case, you may be wondering where this leaves you and what are your next steps. Well done on reaching this point in your decision-making. Rest assured, there are things that you can do to support you. To help you to progress, it may be important for you to work out what support you need. Ask yourself, what questions do I have unanswered?

Your answer to this question may help you to highlight the type of support that you would like:

• Other self-employed friends or colleagues – they may be able to provide a reality check on what it is like to be self-employed.

• Other friends or colleagues – they may be able to provide a sounding board to hear your questions and offer practical, technical and emotional support.

• A professional coach – they may be able to provide professional support and guidance to help you to make your decision. In particular there is a network of licensed coaches who provide tailored support in helping people transition to self-employment. They are licensed to use the Testing the Water™ questionnaire, which helps you to assess your readiness for self-employment. See about Evolve Enterprise on page 52 for more information.

'Yes, but I still need some support'

For some of us, working through this practical guide may have confirmed that self-employment is for us. However, it may have highlighted some areas of support that we require to make it easier for us to move into self-employment.

Well done on reaching this outcome in your decision-making. If this is the case, it may be important for you to work out what areas of support you would value. Ask yourself, what are the areas where I would like support and guidance?

Your answer to this question may help you to highlight the type of support that you would value:

- Other self-employed friends or colleagues – they may be able to provide answers and personal views to particular questions in relation to being self-employed.

- Other friends or colleagues – they may be able to provide technical, practical and emotional support.

- A professional coach – they may be able to provide professional support in helping you to develop your capability in a specific area. In particular there is a network of licensed coaches who provide tailored support in helping people transition to self-employment. They are able to support individuals in developing their capability in each of the eight factors. Again, they are licensed to use the Testing the Water™ questionnaire, which can support you in the transition to self-employment. See about Evolve Enterprise for more information.

- Other information sources – in **chapter 12. where to go more help** there is a list of relevant information sources. These may be able to provide answers to practical and technical questions.

'Yes, I am ready to go self-employed!'

Finally, for some of us working through this practical guide it may have confirmed that self-employment is definitely for us. It may have also confirmed that we are ready to make that move quite soon.

Well done on reaching this decision. Remember to develop our advice sources to support us on our journey to self-employment. We may need practical, emotional and technical support at different times during our business set up.

A final word

Whatever our decision and wherever we are on our journey to self-employment, we are at the perfect place.

We may have declined the offer of self-employment, or we may be ready to jump in with both feet. For some of us, we may still be in the process of testing the water to see if self-employment is for us. Wherever we are, remember one thing: all around us we have plenty of resources to tap into to support us on our way.

Good luck with your journey and realising your plans, dreams and ambitions.

chapter 12. where to get more help

As well as your own advice sources, there are numerous external sources of information, help and support.

Here is your own personal check-list:

Completed	Support Areas

☐ **Business Support**
Covers a number of areas including tax and insurance and offers 24-hour legal advice to members with small businesses.
Federation of Small Businesses www.fsb.org.uk

☐ **Companies**
If you form a new company, you must agree and register its name with the Registrar of Companies at Companies House.
Companies House - 02920 380 801or visit www.companieshouse.co.uk
Northern Ireland (Companies Registry) – 028 9023 44 88

☐ **Help with computers and IT**
The DTI's UK Online for Business programme aims to help small businesses use information technology to their competitive advantage.
Contact UK Online for Business on 0845 715 2000 or visit www.businesslink.org

☐ **Inland Revenue**
Helpline for Newly Self-Employed – 08459 15 45 15
Business Support Teams, free of charge – 08459 15 45 15
or visit www.inlandrevenue.gov.uk/bst

☐ **Intellectual property**
Grants patents and registers designs, trade-marks and copyrights in the UK.
Patent Office – 01633 813 930
or visit www.patent.gov.uk or www.intellectual-property.gov.uk

☐ **National Insurance contributions**
National Insurance self-employment help-line on 0845 915 4655

☐ **Prince's Trust**
The Prince's Trust provide support and guidance for individuals between 18-30 years old who are looking to set up their own business.
The Prince's Trust - 020 7543 1234 or visit www.princes-trust.org.uk

Completed	Support Areas

Special help for small businesses
The Small Business Service's experienced advisors offer impartial advice to help you plan and implement ideas for improving and growing your business.

England: call Business Link on 0845 600 9006 or visit www.businesslink.org

Wales: call Business Connect on 08457 969798 or visit www.businessconnect.org.uk

Scotland: call Small Business Gateway (Lowlands) on 0845 609 6611 or visit www.sbgateway.com

Highlands & Islands Enterprise: call Business Information Source on 01463 234 171 or visit www.hie.co.uk

Northern Ireland: call Local Enterprise Development Unit (LEDU) on 028 90 491031 or visit www.ledu-ni.gov.uk

VAT
Customs and Excise National Advice Centre on 0845 010 900 or visit www.hmce.gov.uk

Unemployment
Practical advice and support for unemployed people who want to run their own business.
New Deal – 0845 606 2626 or visit www.thesite.org/newdeal/diagram

about Evolve Enterprise

Evolve Enterprise aims to help people make the transition to self-employment.

Central to this is the Testing the Water™ questionnaire, which helps to find out people's readiness to move into self-employment. It can identify areas of strengths and also potential areas to focus on to facilitate the transition to self-employment.

Support is available in the form of:

- One to one coaching with a licensed coach.
- Workshops, which can be arranged for teams and organisations.
- This practical guide.

If you are a coach or career counsellor and would like to be able to use the Testing the Water™ questionnaire with your clients, we run licensing workshops to enable you to do this.

More information is available from www.evolve.eu.com/evolveenterprise

Evolve Enterprise is part of Evolve Consulting Services Limited.

Average processing adjustments for 100 ISO film

Contrast		Processing time %
Highlight 6 stops brighter than Zone III	N - 2	75
Highlight 5 stops brighter than Zone III	N - 1	85
Highlight 3 stops brighter than Zone III	N + 1	130
Highlight 2 stops brighter than Zone III	N + 2	150